THE GREAT ICE AGE

A History from Beginning to End

BY HOURLY HISTORY

Copyright © 2024 by Hourly History.

All rights reserved.

The cover photo is a derivative of "Cave lion at the Ice Age Centre" (https://commons.wikimedia.org/wiki/File:Cave_lion_at_the_Ice_Age_Centre.jpg) by Ice Age Centre, used under CC BY-SA 4.0 (https://creativecommons.org/licenses/by-sa/4.0/deed.en) and "Ice Age Fauna of Northern Spain" (https://commons.wikimedia.org/wiki/File:Ice_age_fauna_of_northern_Spain_-_Mauricio_Ant%C3%B3n.jpg) by Mauricio Antón, used under CC BY 2.5 (https://creativecommons.org/licenses/by/2.5/deed.en), and "Ice Age Earth" (https://commons.wikimedia.org/wiki/File:IceAgeEarth.jpg) by Ittiz, used under CC BY-SA 3.0 (https://creativecommons.org/licenses/by-sa/3.0/deed.en).

Table of Contents

Introduction
The Changing Climate History of Planet Earth
What Causes Ice Ages?
The Pleistocene Epoch
Looking for Evidence
Glaciation During the Great Ice Age
Climate During the Ice Age
Flora and Fauna
Humans during the Ice Age
Has the Ice Age Ended?
Conclusion
Bibliography

Introduction

The Val de Bagnes is a beautiful valley located high in the Swiss Alps. Early in the nineteenth century, geologists became aware that the people who lived there had an odd belief: that the deep striations in the rocks of the valley and the large boulders tumbled along its base were due to the fact that once, the valley had been covered in ice. Obviously, that was rather silly—after all, how could a mountain valley be covered in a layer of ice thick enough to scour the very rocks?

The conventional geological explanation was that the physical evidence obvious in Val de Bagnes and elsewhere had been caused by flooding. Not everyone was convinced though, and a number of geologists believed that only massive swathes of moving ice (glaciers) could account for what was visible. But just how could there have been glaciers that massive in the Swiss Alps?

It wouldn't be until the publication of a seminal book, *Climate and Time in Their Geological Relations*, written by Scottish scientist James Croll in 1875, that the theory would be generally accepted that the climate of planet Earth had gone through a series of cyclic changes with the coldest periods seeing widespread glaciation and the formation of massive ice sheets. These periods of extreme cold became generally known as ice ages.

Given that these climate changes have been accepted by the scientific world for less than 150 years, it's unsurprising that our knowledge of what they involved and how they were caused is still developing. It is now generally agreed that planet Earth has experienced at least five major ice ages. However, research has shown that these ice ages weren't uniformly cold; even during them, there were fluctuations in temperature leading to periods of extreme cold (glacial periods) and periods of warming (interglacial periods) when the ice sheets and glaciers retreated.

Even more startlingly, research has shown that we are still in an ice age today, one that began more than 2.5 million years ago, though we are currently experiencing one of the warmer interglacial periods. Ice ages weren't just a feature of Earth's ancient history; they are relevant to us all today, and an understanding of what causes these fluctuations and when we may expect the current interglaciation to end is a topic of direct and current relevance.

Let's take a look at what we know about the most recent ice age, commonly known as the Great Ice Age.

Chapter One

The Changing Climate History of Planet Earth

"We definitely don't want to go through another Ice Age or another natural cycle of global warming."

—David Grinspoon

The notion of large-scale changes in the climate of Earth began to gain acceptance in the nineteenth century. Climate change wasn't a simple thing for many of the mainly Christian scientists of the period to accept. Until that time, most scientists assumed that the Earth had experienced a period of gradual but steady cooling since it was first created.

Some felt that to suggest that Earth had a history that was almost inconceivably ancient and which had included periods when large parts of the planet were covered in ice was blasphemous. After all, the Bible gave a detailed account of the creation of the Earth, and it didn't mention ice ages at all, only a single catastrophic flood. Some felt that to believe in a planet that was perhaps billions of years old and that had experienced dramatic climate fluctuations was fundamentally wrong. In its own way, the theory of ice ages was almost as controversial as Charles Darwin's theory of evolution, which also emerged during the nineteenth century.

As the evidence accumulated during the late nineteenth and early twentieth centuries, it became more difficult to deny that glaciers once covered much of what are today inhabited, agricultural, and rural areas, including the locations of major cities. This evidence confirmed that there have been at least five major ice ages during the history of the Earth. These have been identified as the Huronian (2.5 to 2.2 billion years ago), the Cryogenian (720 to 635 million years ago), the Early Paleozoic (460 to 420 million years ago), the Late Paleozoic (360 to 255 million years ago), and the Pleistocene. The Pleistocene Ice Age began around 2.5 million years ago and continues to the present day. It is commonly referred to as the Great Ice Age or simply the Ice Age.

The thing that characterizes these ages is glaciation—the spread of glaciers and ice sheets. It may be worth pausing to define just what a glacier is. Glaciers are actually nothing more than vast accumulations of snow. As the snow builds up, its weight causes the lower levels to be compacted into a solid mass of ice. During glacial periods, these glaciers increase in size, and in warmer interglacial periods, they get a little smaller each year. When they are growing, gradually, almost imperceptibly, glaciers flow outward under the weight of accumulating snow. In valleys, they flow down through the valley toward the sea. Large continental ice sheets gradually expand in all directions.

Glaciers are a rich source of organic material. Plant and animal material is trapped within the ice as the glaciers move, and this material is preserved to be released once more when the ice finally melts. Glaciers have enormous power. As they move, they scour the landscape beneath them, gouging rocks and displacing huge boulders. The zenith of any ice age is measured by the extent of ice coverage on the surface of the Earth, with the peak coverage being known as the glacial maximum. During the glacial maximum of the most recent glacial period, which occurred around 20,000 years ago, it is believed that up to 25% of the total land area of our planet was covered in glaciers and ice sheets. Because so much water was locked up in glaciers during this time, the sea level was about 400 feet (120 meters) lower than it is today.

The periods between ice ages are known as greenhouse periods, and these are defined as times when there are no continental glaciers anywhere on Earth. During these periods, sea levels rise, and levels of carbon dioxide, methane, and other greenhouse gases in the atmosphere are notably higher. It is believed that Earth has experienced greenhouse periods for over 80% of its history.

What's particularly notable is that, during both ice ages and greenhouse periods, the climate is not stable. During ice ages, there are times when glaciers are advancing and retreating, and during greenhouse periods, the average temperature and the level of greenhouse gases in the atmosphere fluctuate. It's also clear that even these fluctuations are not constant across the whole planet; the northern and southern hemispheres experience different rates and extents of warming and cooling.

So, when we talk about both warmer and cooler periods in the history of our planet, it's important to remember that these weren't consistent. In human terms, the climate may seem to be something fixed or susceptible to only gradual change, but in terms of geologic history, paleoclimatology (the study of climate in times before measuring instruments were available) shows that the climate is something that has always been in a state of change. The issue that has increasingly driven paleoclimatology is trying to understand what it is that brings these changes about.

Chapter Two

What Causes Ice Ages?

"I think people today just have the expectation that we deserve a perfectly benign climate forever."

—Hugh Ross

The climate is subject to a bewildering number of variables, and understanding these and their complex interrelationships continues to be a challenge for scientists. One factor that seems to be involved is fluctuations in the Earth's orbit around the sun. These fluctuations vary across a span of millions, or perhaps tens of millions of years, in several important ways.

The orbit itself varies (eccentricity), meaning that the Earth may be further from or closer to the sun at different times. The way in which the Earth tilts as it orbits (obliquity) provides a variation in the way in which the polar ice caps are exposed to sunlight. The Earth also wobbles in its orbit (precession), again bringing a variation in the amount of sun that reaches the poles.

These periodic fluctuations in the amount of solar energy reaching the Earth are called Milankovitch cycles, named after the Serbian geophysicist and astronomer Milutin Milankovic, who first described them in the 1920s. When this astronomical description of ice ages was first suggested, it was widely seen as being a full explanation for these massive climate shifts, but more recent research indicates that while the astronomical explanation is certainly a factor, the cause of ice ages is much more complex and may involve a number of other factors.

As techniques for obtaining and analyzing core samples from the Earth's subsurface became more advanced, it became increasingly clear that there was some form of relationship between the amount of greenhouse gases (carbon dioxide, methane, and ozone, for example) in the atmosphere and the warming of the climate. For example, during the current Ice Age, core samples showed that there were higher concentrations of greenhouse gases during interglacial periods and lower concentrations during glacial periods.

Still, there was a fundamental and unanswered question: were these increases in greenhouse gases caused by the ice age, or did an increase in such gases cause global warming and cause ice ages to end? Obviously, that's an important question and one of pressing interest to climatologists trying to understand the period of warming that we are currently experiencing.

Until relatively recently, most climatologists believed that increasing greenhouse gases were caused by global warming, but new research suggests that this may not be the case. In a study published in *Nature* magazine, a team of scientists led by Jeremy Shakun, associate professor at the Department of Earth and Environmental Sciences at Boston College, analyzed a large number of core samples and concluded that global warming lagged behind an increase in greenhouse gases by a factor of several hundred years. This finding strongly suggested that rising greenhouse gases were the cause of warming rather than being caused by it.

However, the study also showed that there was a brief period of warming before the first rise in greenhouse gases, suggesting that perhaps this first warming led to the release of greenhouse gases that then accelerated the continued warming. Just like the astronomical description, it is now clear that there is a direct relationship between the volume of greenhouse gases in the atmosphere and the climate, but it seems unlikely that this provides a single explanation for ice ages. There is also no complete answer to just where the increasing levels of, for example, carbon dioxide came from. Today, the burning of fossil fuels, deforestation, and other human activities contribute to the increase of greenhouse gases in the atmosphere, but the samples analyzed by the team at Boston College came from more than 20,000 years ago, long before human beings could have had any impact on the climate.

Then there are plate tectonics. The surface of the Earth may feel stable beneath your feet, but actually, it is a series of enormous plates that float on top of a layer of molten rock. These plates move very slowly, but their movement and particularly areas where they collide are thought to cause climate change. Even the continents themselves move in a process known as continental drift. The proximity of the continents (particularly North America and Eurasia) to the North Pole is thought to have a major impact on glaciation and interglaciation.

The oceans also play a major role in the Earth's climate. Circulation of warmed water at the Equator to other areas is an important mechanism where heat is transferred from the Equator toward the poles. Oceanic circulation is affected directly by both tectonic movement and continental drift. Effective circulation requires oceanic pathways through which the seas can circulate to distribute heat. As continents drift further apart, these pathways increase, causing heat transfer to also increase. Conversely, if tectonic movement decreases the size of these routes, heat transfer decreases. In addition, ocean circulation and the transfer of heat seem to release carbon dioxide into the atmosphere, which may accelerate warming and deglaciation. As warming occurs, the ice caps begin to melt, releasing vast quantities of fresh water, which may interrupt or even change the pattern of ocean currents.

Volcanic activity has probably also played a significant role in climate change during the long history of the Earth. Volcanoes spew out a vast amount of carbon and sulfur dioxide when they erupt. When Mount Pinatubo in the Philippines erupted in 1991, it created a cloud of sulfur dioxide estimated at more than 20 million metric tons. This single eruption was thought to have been the cause of an average temperature drop that reached 1 degree Fahrenheit (0.5 degrees Celsius) across the whole planet for a period of three years. There have been times during the history of Earth when there have been high levels of volcanic activity, and it is believed that these have contributed to major climate fluctuations.

The effects of all these disparate factors are further influenced by positive feedback. The reflectivity of the Earth (albedo) influences the volume of sunlight that is absorbed or reflected back. As ice sheets spread, they increase the overall reflectivity of the planet, which means that more of the sun's energy is reflected back into the atmosphere. This leads to cooling, which may produce more ice, which increases reflectivity and promotes the further spread of ice. Conversely, as ice sheets recede, reflectivity decreases and more of the sun's energy is absorbed, leading temperatures to increase and the ice sheets to recede further.

Just like the factors that cause ice ages, the mechanisms that lead to the end of an ice age are not fully understood. Research generally seems to show that in the Middle and Late Pleistocene, long-term cycles that lasted around 100,000 years characterized warming and cooling. Within these long cycles, there were shorter periods of glaciation and deglaciation that saw glaciers and ice sheets advancing and receding.

The Last Glacial Maximum occurred around 20,000 years ago. Since that time, the temperature on Earth has been generally rising, and the ice has been receding. But not consistently. A study of core samples tells us that this warming was interrupted abruptly toward the end of the Late Pleistocene, around 12,800 years ago. This period, known as the Younger Dryas, lasted for almost 1,200 years and saw a period of cooling where temperatures dropped by up to 14 degrees Fahrenheit (8 degrees Celsius). The Younger Dryas was a global phenomenon, and it ended as abruptly as it had begun as the temperature resumed its gradual climb. This was, in geological terms, a very recent event, yet we have absolutely no idea what caused this short but intense period of cooling.

Perhaps it's worth pointing out here that ice ages are very unusual in the long history of our planet. Over the course of four and a half billion years, there have been only about five ice ages in Earth's history, separated by periods of hundreds of millions of years when the global climate has been relatively stable and temperatures higher (greenhouse periods). Ice ages are periods of rapid change where the climate oscillates between warming and cooling. There are a number of factors involved, with the most obvious being the relative position of the Earth to the sun, but this alone doesn't explain these rapid changes.

This is, of course, a very brief look at some of the factors that are currently believed to play a role in climate change. They are extremely complex, particularly in relation to one another. In simple terms, there does not seem to be any single cause of ice ages or greenhouse periods. These appear to be the result of a number of factors, and the precise way in which these relate is still a matter of debate among climatologists and scientists. Part of the problem is that we lack data from our ancient past. Fortunately, in terms of the Pleistocene Epoch, we do have access to more detailed information that helps to provide a more accurate picture of what occurred in Earth's recent history.

Chapter Three

The Pleistocene Epoch

"Without the death of forests by Ice Age advance, there would be no northern lakes."

—Michael Dowd

The geological period known as the Pleistocene was first named in 1839 by Scottish geologist Charles Lyell. The name comes from Greek and means "newest." Lyell used this name to distinguish geologic formations he had found in Sicily from the preceding epoch, the Pliocene ("recent"), also named by Lyell in the 1830s. The geological epoch in which we currently live, the Holocene, followed directly after the Pleistocene and is generally accepted to have begun around 11,700 years ago when the last glacial period ended.

When Lyell gave the Pleistocene its name, it was generally accepted to have begun somewhere around 1.8 million years ago. This dating was repeatedly challenged in the nineteenth century, and in 2009, the International Union of Geological Sciences announced that the date marking the boundary between the Pliocene and Pleistocene had been moved back to around 2.5 million years ago.

The Pleistocene is often known as the Great Ice Age or simply the Ice Age (though as we have seen, the Pleistocene is just one of a number of ice ages that Earth has experienced) because it has seen several cycles of glaciation and interglaciation. The preceding Pliocene Epoch was marked by a gradual increase in global temperature and by the spread of forests and grasslands.

Toward the end of the Pliocene, the continents of North and South America, which had previously been separated, were joined at the Isthmus of Panama. As explained in the preceding chapter, this may have caused significant changes in oceanic circulation, which in turn may have been involved in the general drop in temperatures that began with the Pleistocene. Early climatologists believed that the Great Ice Age had ended with the beginning of the Holocene Epoch, but we now know that not to be true. The current warm period is simply an interglacial interlude in a continuing ice age.

The Pleistocene Epoch is often subdivided into three periods: the Early, Mid, and Late. During the Early Pleistocene, there was a regular fluctuation in the extent of glaciers and ice sheets that followed a cycle of approximately 41,000 years. These seemed to have a direct relationship to Milankovitch cycles and followed periodic fluctuations in the orbit of the Earth around the sun.

Then, around 1.2 million years ago, there was a notable change, often called the Mid-Pleistocene Transition. After this point, the fluctuations and interglacial periods were no longer regular, and very large ice sheets formed over parts of the planet, though major glacial and interglacial periods seemed to occur around every 100,000 years. It has also been noted that this period was marked by a drop in atmospheric carbon dioxide, perhaps due to a decline in volcanic activity, and that this may have been a factor in the drastic change.

The Late Pleistocene began approximately 130,000 years ago and continued to the beginning of the Holocene Epoch 11,700 years ago. The Late Pleistocene was marked by the rapid spread of glaciers, which reached their maximum extent around 20,000 years ago. This was a time when the flora and fauna of the Earth were going through massive changes.

The Late Pleistocene was marked by what is known as the Quaternary extinction event. Many of the world's large animals (megafauna) became extinct, including species such as the woolly mammoth, mastodon, woolly rhinoceros, ground sloth, saber-toothed cat, and the stegodon. Most of the species that became extinct were large herbivores, though this led in turn to the extinction of some of the carnivores that preyed upon them. However, it wasn't just the changes in habitat caused by erratic cycles of warming and cooling that led to the extinction of all these creatures. During this period, a new species had emerged that would prove fearsomely good at hunting: humans.

The first archaic humans of the genus *Homo* seem to have emerged in the Early Pleistocene, probably in present-day Africa. The first *Homo sapiens* are thought to have begun to appear around 300,000 years ago. They shared the Late Pleistocene with another even older hominid species, *Homo neanderthalensis* (Neanderthals). While *Homo sapiens* proliferated and spread out across Eurasia from Africa, Neanderthals became extinct toward the end of the Late Pleistocene, around 40,000 years ago.

Scientists have come to believe that the relatively sudden extinction of so many species of large herbivores during the Late Pleistocene was probably only partly due to climate change but also partly due to hunting by the first groups of human hunter-gatherers. Those nomadic groups moved according to whether the glaciers were advancing or retreating, moving north during interglacial periods and moving back to temperate lands closer to the Equator during glacial periods.

As the ice sheets retreated, they left a bare landscape filled with large numbers of lakes and marshes created by water running off melting glaciers. Gradually, upland areas would become grasslands with a few larch and spruce trees. At the margins of glacial areas, tundra would have developed, with a few isolated trees, grasses, sedges, and herbaceous vegetation. Lower areas would have become vast spruce forests and wetlands dominated by semi-aquatic plant life. Temperatures in both summer and winter were generally cooler than today, though not significantly so, and this would have been a landscape that was generally wet, with more rainfall than we see today.

The newly revealed lands left by retreating glaciers, through which our human ancestors roamed in search of food, differed in terms of flora and fauna from those seen in the same regions today. The land masses of the Earth were also very different. With so much water locked into glaciers and continental ice sheets, sea levels were significantly lower than they are today. Estimates suggest that sea levels at the Last Glacial Maximum may have been 400 feet (120 meters) lower than they are today. That meant that areas that are presently under the sea were then part of the continents.

For example, today, Siberia and Alaska are separated by a body of water, the Bering Strait. In the Late Pleistocene, this was an area of plains that is now known as the Bering Land Bridge. It was by crossing this piece of land, revealed as the ice sheets melted but before sea levels rose sufficiently to cover it, that our distant ancestors first reached what is now North America. As the glaciers continued to melt, sea levels rose, and the humans who would go on to inhabit all of North, Central, and South America were isolated from Eurasia. Likewise, human settlers from New Guinea would have been able to walk to what is today Australia, and humans from Africa would have been able to walk over what is today the English Channel to reach Britain before rising sea levels cut them off from the lands from which they had come.

This constantly changing landscape, particularly in the last 20,000 years, led to the expansion of human societies and the occupation of new lands that were being revealed by melting glaciers. Then, as glaciers and ice sheets continued to melt, some of these new lands were inundated as sea levels rose. The early history of the human race was directly connected to and influenced by the cyclical expansion and contraction of glaciers and ice sheets during the Pleistocene.

Clearly, this early human history took place long before there were written records or any ability to record details of the climate or landscape. So, how do we know what these looked like during the Pleistocene?

Chapter Four

Looking for Evidence

"The epoch of intense cold which preceded the present creation has been only a temporary oscillation of the earth's temperature."

—Louis Agassiz

The first scientists to postulate that large parts of the Earth had once been covered by ice were influenced simply by looking at the landscape in certain areas. In many valleys, there were huge boulders, called erratics, that had been transported from their original bedrock by some enormous force. Many valleys also displayed the presence of smaller areas of debris that had been scoured from the valley sides, leaving large piles of tumbled rock known as moraines. These could be seen in many parts of Europe, including Scotland, Scandinavia, Switzerland, and France, as well as in Canada and the northern United States. Obviously, something had once happened to create these effects, but just what was it?

For a long time, some form of flooding was thought to be the cause, which neatly tied in with the biblical account of a world-changing flood. Not all scientists were convinced though; some of the erratics weighed thousands of tons, far too heavy to be moved by water. Glaciers still existed in, for example, some parts of the Alps, and the terrain in other ice-free parts of the world looked very similar to valleys that had been revealed as these glaciers retreated. For the first time, people began to wonder whether, at some point in the distant past, much larger areas of the Earth had been covered by continental ice sheets and glaciers.

That made sense, but it was also clear that evidence of glaciers scouring the landscape below was not present everywhere. In Alaska, for example, there was no such evidence. By mapping the areas where these features occur, scientists were able to envisage not a single sheet of ice that covered much of the northern hemisphere (which was what the first theorists had thought) but a series of centers of ice accumulation from which giant glaciers were extruded into valleys. These occurred only in areas where it wasn't just cold but where there were also high levels of snowfall. The lack of evidence of glacial action in Alaska, for example, was because this area did not have sufficient snowfall to create and sustain glaciers.

Then, the remains of river channels were discovered under the sea. The Hudson River in the United States, for example, has scoured a deep channel through the landscape of eastern New York State. It was discovered that this scoured channel extends far out to sea on the continental shelf. Rivers can't scour channels after they enter the sea, so the only possible conclusion was that once, the sea level had been much, much lower than it is today. That could be explained if a great deal of water was locked into ice sheets and glaciers, and this discovery gave added weight to the notion of an ice age.

Then, scientists began to recover core samples from beneath the Earth's surface. Some of the most significant were taken from the seabed around the island of Barbados. These samples showed that coral had grown at different levels in the ancient past. Coral can only live close to the surface of the ocean, so this allowed scientists to fix the sea level in the ancient past and to chart its erratic rise over thousands of years. This too confirmed the gradual and inconsistent melting of ice as contributing significantly to a change in sea level. These discoveries helped the theory of ice ages to be accepted, but it wasn't until relatively recently that new technology allowed much more detailed analysis of ice age samples.

Probably the most important of these sediment core samples were recovered in 2008 and 2009 by a team from the Continental Scientific Drilling Program (a multinational geoscience program) from Lake Elgygytgyn, a Siberian lake located some 60 miles (100 kilometers) north of the Arctic Circle. This lake is actually a meteorite crater that was filled with water from melting glaciers, and the samples recovered there have provided a snapshot of a great deal of the Pleistocene Epoch.

These core samples revealed something entirely unexpected; during the Pleistocene, there were uncharacteristic warm periods when the temperature at Lake Elgygytgyn was significantly higher than it is today—perhaps 9 degrees Fahrenheit (5 degrees Celsius) higher than present temperatures. These periods have been called super interglacials, and so far, we have no explanation for them. It has been noted that these periods of warming correspond to extensive deglaciation in other parts of the world including Antarctica, suggesting that these were global rather than local events. The same samples contain pollen, which helps us to form a picture of what the landscape in this area may have looked like in ancient times.

Ice cores, samples taken from deep beneath the Arctic and Antarctic ice sheets, also tell us a great deal about things like global temperature and the presence of higher or lower levels of greenhouse gases. Deep sea sediment core samples help us to understand oceanic circulation—how it has changed and how this has influenced the world's climate.

Given that the theory of ice ages has only been widely accepted for around 150 years, we have made astounding progress not only in confirming their occurrence but also in understanding their impact. Moreover, we are beginning to comprehend at least some of the causes. Still, this is very much an area of emerging knowledge. New technologies and new approaches mean that there are probably many more surprises in store for those who seek to understand the Great Ice Age.

Chapter Five

Glaciation During the Great Ice Age

"The threat of a new ice age must now stand alongside nuclear war as a likely source of wholesale death and misery for mankind."

—Nigel Calder

The span of 2.5 million years—the period covering the Pleistocene Epoch—may seem an unimaginable gulf of time to humans, but it is barely a single moment in the history of planet Earth. We now know that during this short period, our planet has been affected by rapid and frequent oscillations of the global climate. These changes caused episodes that saw the advance and retreat of glaciers of vast size in the northern hemisphere, which in turn transformed the landscape and the oceans. Precisely how many glacial and interglacial periods occurred during the Pleistocene is still a matter of debate and definition, but it's generally accepted that there must have been at least 20 such episodes of warming and cooling. But just how great was the extent of glaciation, and how much ice covered the land? This is a question that has proved very difficult to answer with any degree of certainty.

The extent of glaciers is relatively easy to infer because their effects on the landscape are so obvious. We can conclude from this that, for example, during the periods of maximum glaciation, Scotland, most of Scandinavia, continental Russia as far south as the city of Moscow, and all of Canada and North America as far south as the cities of Chicago and Detroit would have been covered by glaciers. The Last Glacial Maximum of the Pleistocene took place approximately 20,000 years ago. This was a significant maximum, with glaciers reaching 90% of the maximum extent they had achieved during the previous one million years.

Just how deep were the ice sheets and glaciers that formed during periods of glaciation? It's very difficult to be certain—after all, when ice melts, it leaves no visible clues as to how thick it once was. Most estimates suggest that parts of the ice sheets were over one mile (1.6 kilometers) thick. In parts of Northern Europe and Canada, the weight of ice was so great that it actually pressed the rock of the Earth's crust down into the softer mantle below. When the ice finally melted, these rocks began to rise again, something they have been doing for around the last ten thousand years, leaving beaches far above the sea, not because the sea level has fallen, but because the land is rising without the weight of ice pressing down on it. Finland, for example, gains about 2.7 square miles (4.3 square kilometers) of surface area every year because of this phenomenon.

During periods of maximum glaciation, ice covered over 17 million square miles (44 million square kilometers), more than 25% of the total land mass of the Earth. In addition to centers of ice accumulation in Greenland and the Antarctic, there were two major ice sheets, both in the northern hemisphere. In Canada and North America, ice covered a vast area as far south as southern Illinois. There were also other smaller ice centers that reached as far south as the mountains of Mexico. In Eurasia, an ice center covered much of Scandinavia as well as large parts of the British Isles, though there were also glaciers in areas of Germany, Poland, Russia, Switzerland, and Austria.

In some places, glaciers seem to have reached as far as the Equator, with evidence of glaciation being seen in the mountains of Africa. The famous snows of Mount Kilimanjaro in Tanzania are actually the last remains of one such glacier. Glaciation was less pronounced in the southern hemisphere, though there is clear evidence of glaciation in both New Zealand and Tasmania.

Some of the ice in glaciers that exist today was formed during the Pleistocene. Glaciers in the Himalayas, for example, are believed to contain ice that was first formed hundreds of thousands of years ago. In many cases, these ice centers became zones from which glaciers gradually spread. As they moved, the glaciers scoured material from the landscape below and pushed it before them. This process led to some fundamental changes in the landscape.

Areas such as the northern Great Plains of America, the flat plains of central Germany and part of Poland, and the plains of parts of Russia were created by glaciers pushing unimaginable quantities of till, rock fragments, and clay in front of them. The upland areas over which the glaciers passed, on the other hand, were left largely barren, punctuated by large lakes when melting ice-filled features in the rock. A great deal of the landscape of the northern hemisphere was directly created by, or at least influenced by, glaciation during the Pleistocene Epoch.

Chapter Six

Climate During the Ice Age

"Civilization is the interval between Ice Ages."

—Will Durant

As you will now be aware, there is no such thing as an average climate here on planet Earth. For most of the history of our planet, the climate has been in a state of flux, cycling between warmer and cooler periods for reasons that we still don't fully understand. Even the relatively recent Pleistocene Epoch saw a range of such oscillations. Even though this period is generally known as the Great Ice Age, it involved times when the average temperature was higher than it is today! So, when we are talking about the climate during the Pleistocene, it's important to remember that this was not constant or consistent.

What we do know is that during periods of glaciation, the temperature was generally cooler, and this also seems to have coincided with a lower concentration of greenhouse gases in the atmosphere, though there is no agreement on why this happened. Even within glacial and interglacial periods, there were abrupt and unexplained changes in global climate.

For example, the Last Interglacial Period extended from around 130,000 to 115,000 years ago and was punctuated by three unexplained periods during which the global temperature abruptly dropped. This was followed by the Last Glacial Period (sometimes colloquially known as the Last Ice Age), which lasted from 115,000 to 11,700 years ago. Even this period of cold was punctuated by more than 20 examples of warming, known as interstadials. Thus, even in the relatively short period since *Homo sapiens* first emerged, the climate has been going through repeated and extreme changes.

In general, and accepting these many variations, the Pleistocene was distinctly different from the preceding Pliocene in terms of climate. Whereas the climate during the Pliocene was generally humid and warm, the climate during the Pleistocene was cooler and much more arid. This transformation of the climate brought profound changes in the landscape and ecosystems across the world. Where vast forests had predominated in the Pliocene, these were greatly reduced during the Pleistocene, with grasslands and tundra at glacier margins becoming more common. Yet even this wasn't consistent.

Probably the most important takeaway here is that there wasn't a consistent climate during the Pleistocene Epoch. The last two and a half million years have seen almost continual climate change, from the cold periods during glacial maximums to times when the average temperature was higher than it is today. These fluctuations caused large-scale changes to the ecosystems on Earth and to the plants and animals that inhabited them.

Chapter Seven

Flora and Fauna

"The climate of this planet has been changing since God put the planet here."

—James Spann

The generally cooler temperatures during the Pleistocene led to the evolution of a number of large mammal species that were uniquely adapted to living in areas on the margins of glaciers that were subject to annual thawing and re-freezing (periglacial areas). Mammals were already an ancient group of animals by the time that the Pleistocene began. Up to the time of the extinction of the dinosaurs around 65 million years ago, mammals were generally small, with few exceeding two pounds (one kilogram) in weight. Within 20 million years of the extinction of dinosaurs, mammals evolved that were up to one thousand times larger. The evolution of large mammals continued during the Pleistocene, with the appearance of new species uniquely suited to living in a cooler environment.

Probably the best-known large mammal of the Pleistocene was the woolly mammoth (*Mammuthus primigenius*). This animal, a relative of the Asian elephant, began to evolve during the Pleistocene in Siberia around 800,000 years ago. The woolly mammoth was well suited to life in the periglacial areas, as it was covered in a coat of dense fur. Adults could grow to weigh more than eight metric tons and live up to sixty years. These creatures thrived in their environment, and vast herds probably roamed the steppes of Eurasia and North America.

We know more about these animals than many other extinct species because we have more than just fossil remains to examine. Carcasses of woolly mammoths have been recovered from ice sheets, and many bones, teeth, and tusks have survived. In fact, the woolly mammoth didn't become extinct until around 4,000 years ago when the last examples died on Wrangel Island in Russia.

The woolly mammoths weren't the only large herbivores to roam the landscapes of the Late Pleistocene. The woolly rhinoceros probably derived from a creature that evolved during the Pliocene, and this too was truly massive; males were more than ten feet (three meters) long and weighed up to two metric tons. Like the woolly mammoth, this animal lived in periglacial areas, though remains have also been discovered in more temperate areas. The woolly rhinoceros appears to have become extinct around 14,000 years ago, during an interstadial warming period known as the Bølling-Allerød warming. While we cannot be certain, it seems likely that this relatively short warming period changed the habitats in which the woolly rhinoceros lived and that this may have led to its extinction.

Other now-extinct Pleistocene herbivores included the giant armadillo (*Glyptodon*) and the giant sloth (*Megatherium*). Pleistocene herbivores weren't only found in periglacial areas. In temperate zones too, new large mammals evolved. These included the mastodon, another relative of the modern elephant that first appeared before the Pleistocene. During this epoch, these massive creatures (they had an average weight of eight metric tons) inhabited the forests of temperate zones and roamed in vast herds across Eurasia and North America. Even rodents grew to an amazing size during the Pleistocene. The giant beaver, found mainly in North America, was almost as large as some modern bears, with some examples reaching a length of well over seven feet (two meters) from nose to tail.

Not all Pleistocene mammals were peaceful herbivores. *Smilodon* is now often called the saber-toothed tiger, though it wasn't closely related to modern tigers or to any other existing cats. This ferocious predator mainly inhabited the Americas and could grow to weigh over 800 pounds (360 kilograms) and to stand almost four feet (1.2 meters) high at the shoulders. These apex predators preyed on the abundant herds of herbivores during the Pleistocene. They became extinct around 10,000 years ago, probably as a direct result of the disappearance of the herbivores that they hunted.

Another ferocious creature of the Pleistocene was the giant short-faced bear (*Arctodus*). These massive creatures stood almost 6 feet (2 meters) tall and could weigh over 2,000 pounds (900 kilograms)! These bears were omnivores, eating both vegetation and hunting herbivores such as elk and ox. These creatures finally became extinct around 12,000 years ago, most probably due to habitat changes brought about by rising temperatures.

Ecosystems during the Pleistocene varied as glaciers advanced and then retreated. On the margins of glaciers, there was the periglacial area which, in Eurasia, extended for many hundreds of miles south of the margins of the glaciers themselves. Temperatures here were uniformly low, and there was probably permafrost (permanently frozen ground) in much of this area. Further south, there were vast areas of open grassland with relatively few trees. Only in temperate zones, further south still, were there boreal forests of any size, mainly comprising spruce and pine.

Ecosystems during the Pleistocene were directly related to their proximity to the glaciers and ice sheets. Only more distant areas were truly temperate and because this epoch saw almost constant change in the position and extent of ice, these habitats were subject to continual variation. The Pleistocene saw the emergence and spread of a number of large mammal species across all ecosystems, but there was one mammal that first appeared during this epoch that would go on to dominate not just every form of ecosystem but the planet itself: *Homo sapiens*.

Chapter Eight

Humans during the Ice Age

"An Ice Age is coming and I welcome it as much-needed changing."

—David Foreman

The original *Homo* species was *Homo erectus*, which seems to have appeared somewhere around two million years ago, during the Early Pleistocene. *Homo heidelbergensis*, the first mammal species to display most of the features of modern humans, emerged around 600,000 years ago, during the Middle Pleistocene. *Homo heidelbergensis* had a larger brain capacity than other hominid ancestors as well as smaller teeth and a less sloping face. At least two new species evolved from these early ancestors, *Homo neanderthalensis* (Neanderthals) and our own species, *Homo sapiens*. The oldest fossil records for *Homo sapiens* have been found in Africa dating back to around 300,000 years ago, though the species may have developed before that time.

Homo sapiens were distinguished by having a larger brain capacity than any predecessor hominid and a forehead that was close to vertical rather than sloping backward. They were also much more lightly built than previous hominids. Neanderthals were once thought to have been a sub-species of *Homo sapiens*, but more recent studies now suggest that it was a completely separate species, though probably descending from a common ancestor.

Neanderthals emerged at around the same time as *Homo sapiens*, and for a great deal of the Middle and Late Pleistocene, these two hominid species seemed to co-exist. Around 40,000 years ago, Neanderthals became extinct, though we aren't sure why. They seemed to have societies and tools that were just as advanced as those of *Homo sapiens*, and there is no evidence of violence between the species. Nevertheless, by the Late Pleistocene, *Homo sapiens* had become the only species of humans on the planet.

It is believed that these early humans evolved in areas close to the Equator in what is present-day Africa. That certainly makes sense—the temperate zone close to the Equator was less susceptible to climate change caused by glaciation and interglaciation and would have provided a much more consistent and pleasant environment in which to live.

Nevertheless, the fossil evidence makes it clear that early humans soon began to spread out from Africa, though they proved just as vulnerable to the fluctuations of the Ice Age as every other species with which they shared the planet. As the population of humans grew, competition for food resources would have become more intense, leading groups to explore new areas to find food. Evidence of the existence of *Homo sapiens* in Asia has been dated to 270,000 years ago, and finds in South Africa and other areas strongly support the theory that *Homo sapiens* began to migrate from Africa during the period of interglaciation.

However, changes in climate seem to have doomed these early human settlers, and most *Homo sapiens* populations outside Africa seem to have died out by around 100,000 years ago. Large-scale expansion outside this area then began again between 70,000 and 50,000 years ago in what is called the "recent out-of-Africa migration." This time, the new human colonies persisted despite a new glacial maximum around 20,000 years ago. Indeed, many of the humans emerging from Africa took advantage of the falling sea levels caused by the increase of ice sheets and glaciers to travel to lands that had previously been inaccessible, including the Americas, Australia, and the British Isles.

As *Homo sapiens* thrived in almost all areas of the world despite the changing conditions, other large mammals suffered from a series of extinctions. In North America, for example, over 32 species of large mammals disappeared completely in a period of little more than 2,000 years, around the end of the Pleistocene. This included wild horses that had previously been present in large numbers (the horses that later became common in North America were imported from Europe as the native horse population had become extinct) and even giant *Teratornis*, massive birds of prey with wingspans of up to 25 feet (7.5 meters).

The fact that these extinctions (and similar events took place around the world) coincided with the arrival of *Homo sapiens* and their development of tools and hunting weapons has led to a suggestion that at least some of the species were driven to extinction due to over-hunting by humans, though the evidence for this is far from conclusive. While it is certainly true that many large species vanished as humans spread to every part of the world, scientists have suggested that the number of humans involved and the relative crudity of their tools and weapons make it unlikely that they could have been responsible for the disappearance of so many species within a relatively short period.

If humans didn't drive the woolly mammoth and other large species to extinction, what did? These species had successfully survived several episodes of glaciation and interglaciation, so it seems unlikely that climate change alone was responsible. The rapid spread of a disease has been postulated, though to date, there is no evidence to confirm this, and given the range of species involved, a single disease capable of inter-species spread seems unlikely.

All we can be certain of is that, during the Late Pleistocene, megafauna suffered an extinction rate that saw 65% of all species becoming extinct across the world. In some areas (Australia, for example), the extinction rate among large mammals exceeded 80%. These extinctions were also unique (as far as we know) in that previous large-scale extinctions had always led to a process called ecological succession, where new species evolved to fill the gaps left by extinctions. That didn't happen during the Late Pleistocene. Almost no new species seem to have emerged after this wave of extinctions, and space within ecosystems was instead filled by the expansion of existing species.

By the end of the Pleistocene, *Homo sapiens* was the only surviving human species. These early people lived in small groups, probably of no more than a few dozen people. These groups were nomadic, moving annually to follow game animals and to gather nuts and fruit. Agriculture was unknown, and crude tools were made from stone to create knives, axes, and spears.

Homo sapiens survived the Ice Age through its remarkable adaptability. One of the key strategies for survival was the development of clothing made from the skins and furs of animals, which provided necessary protection from the cold. In addition to wearing warm clothing, humans built shelters. These ranged from caves to huts made of mammoth bones and structures insulated with mud, stone, and animal hides to keep the cold at bay.

Control of fire was, of course, a huge advantage that humans had over other animals. Fire provided warmth, light, protection from predators, and the means to cook food in order to make it more digestible and nutritious. Over many generations, it's likely that humans also underwent genetic adaptations to the cold, though this process would have been gradual.

Migration was another survival tactic. Some groups migrated to areas with milder climates, while others explored and settled in newly accessible lands as ice sheets expanded. The social structure of living in groups facilitated the sharing of resources, knowledge, and labor, which was essential for survival in extreme conditions. Yes, even in the Late Pleistocene, humans were beginning to cooperate.

Recent evidence has been found in Europe of the large-scale slaughter of buffalo. The killing of animals on this scale would have required large numbers of people, far more than are thought to have existed in the small bands of family members that formed hunter-gatherer bands. This implies a degree of cooperation between hunter-gatherer groups, which in turn suggests a more complex and far-reaching social organization than was previously suspected.

Our ancestors in the Pleistocene may not have lived in cities or towns, but we are beginning to understand that they were far more than small family groups working in isolation. By the end of the Pleistocene, it seems likely that the first human societies were beginning to appear.

Chapter Nine

Has the Ice Age Ended?

"Without a doubt, the warming of the past 100 years has been a welcome respite from a long and deadly Little Ice Age."

—James Taylor

The simple answer is no. Scientists agree that we are living in a warm interglacial period of a major ice age. Just like all other such interglacials, this is a temporary period of warming. At some point, the Earth will most probably see another glacial maximum that will involve glaciers and ice sheets advancing across the continents and sea levels dropping. Analysis of previous glacial and interglacial periods suggests that the next glacial maximum will probably occur around 85,000 years in the future. At the moment, we know of no way to avoid this. If the human race still exists at that time, then it will have to adapt to living in a very different climate.

However, detailed analysis of the climate in the past tells us that these large cycles are punctuated by shorter periods of cooling and warming. Just like glacials and interglacials, we don't know what causes these shorter fluctuations in climate. The most recent such event—called the Little Ice Age—saw regional cooling in the northern hemisphere, particularly in the North Atlantic, that lasted from the sixteenth to the nineteenth century (1816 became known as the "year without a summer" when snow fell in New England in June and crops failed across the world).

These "flip-flops" during periods of overall warming and cooling seem to have been present throughout the history of the Great Ice Age, but they don't seem to have a regular periodicity, so they can't be anticipated. It's certainly possible that we may face one or more of these anomalous periods long before the expected next glacial period.

What does the fact that we are living in an ice age during an interglacial period mean for the human race and the planet? We are living in a period of warming when ice sheets and glaciers retreat and sea levels rise. In that context, newspaper headlines about the disappearance of ice sheets and record-high temperatures aren't surprising; these have been part of every previous interglacial period. In that sense, global warming can be seen as part of a natural cycle and one that we can do little to prevent. Yet this time, for the first time in the long history of the planet, there is a new factor: human activity.

As noted, ancient core samples tell us that there seems to be a direct connection between the concentration of greenhouse gases in the atmosphere and global warming. In the past, these have come from natural sources, including volcanic eruptions. Today, a sizeable proportion of carbon dioxide, one of the main greenhouse gases, comes from the burning of fossil fuels by humans.

There is a natural carbon emission and absorption cycle that happens every year, but over the last 150 years, human activity has begun to add to the natural production of carbon dioxide. The extra cannot be entirely absorbed and remains in the atmosphere. As a result, atmospheric carbon dioxide is currently at the highest level it has been for the last 15 million years. Natural carbon dioxide levels tend to increase fairly slowly. Typically, it has taken anything up to 20,000 years to see an increase of

100 ppm of carbon dioxide in the atmosphere. Thanks to human activity, we have seen such an increase in just the last 120 years.

The most pressing and significant question facing climate scientists is whether these increases in greenhouse gases due to human activity may lead to climate instability. At the moment, there does not appear to be a clear answer. The global temperature is currently rising, glaciers and ice sheets are receding, and sea levels are rising. While this may simply be because we are experiencing a warming interglacial period, it is also possible that emissions caused by human activity are amplifying natural feedback cycles, which may lead to fundamental changes in the climate of our planet.

It's too early to be certain, but it seems logical and prudent to monitor the situation carefully and, where possible, to decrease our greenhouse gas emissions.

Conclusion

In the long history of our planet, ice ages are anomalies. For the vast majority of its history, the climate on Earth has been relatively stable and much warmer than it is today. During an ice age, that stability disappears, and the global climate changes rapidly and unpredictably, which has a fundamental impact on every ecosystem on the planet and on the plants and animals that live there.

Homo sapiens have existed only during the current Ice Age. We have never experienced a long period of a stable and warmer climate. The first humans survived a glacial maximum, mainly by remaining near the Equator. Now, in this warming interglacial period, we inhabit virtually every part of the Earth. Although we take that for granted, it's possible only because large parts of the planet are now ice-free. One day, that will not be so if, as we expect, the next glacial maximum sees the return of ice sheets and glaciers that will cover many of our major cities. On the other hand, if human activity accelerates the warming of this interglacial period, parts of the planet may become uninhabitable due to rising temperatures.

In human terms, the climate appears to be something that is fixed and unchanging. That's understandable given that, even during the relatively rapid changes seen during ice ages, these may take tens of thousands of years to happen. But we are living in an ice age, and one of the few things we can be certain of is that the climate will continue to change as part of a natural cycle. We cannot be certain how human activity will impact these changes, but it is very possible that it will.

Climate change is one of the most pressing issues currently facing the human race. While climate change could impact every part of our daily lives and those of our descendants, it is an inherent part of the planet on which we live. One of the few things we can say with certainty about the climate is that in one thousand years, it will not be the same as it is now. The detailed study of the ancient history of the current ice age helps us to understand what those changes may look like and how they take place.

That's why the study of the Great Ice Age is so important. It doesn't just tell us about Earth's ancient history and the beginning of the human race, but it also helps us predict what may happen in the future. That could potentially help us to prepare for what may be coming and to devise ways of surviving global climate change as a species.

Bibliography

Chapman, J. A., (1999). *The Great Ice Age: Climate Change and Life.*

Fagan, B. M. (2009). *The Complete Ice Age: How Climate Change Shaped the World.*

Macdougall, D. (2006). *Frozen Earth: The Once and Future Story of Ice Ages.*

Mazur, A. (2022). *Ice Ages: Their Social and Natural History.*

Made in the USA
Coppell, TX
23 June 2024

33814347R10038